ANGER
MANAGEMENT

CW01034224

ANGER
MANAGEMENT

Richard Baxter

Adapted and Paraphrased from
Baxter's *Christian Directory* by
Richard Rushing

THE BANNER OF TRUTH TRUST

THE BANNER OF TRUTH TRUST
3 Murrayfield Road, Edinburgh EH12 6EL, UK
P.O. Box 621, Carlisle, PA 17013, USA

*

© The Banner of Truth Trust 2008

ISBN-13: 978 0 85151 979 1

*

Typeset in 10.5 / 13.5 pt Adobe Caslon Pro
at the Banner of Truth Trust, Edinburgh

Printed in the USA by
Versa Press, Inc.,
East Peoria, IL

ANGER MANAGEMENT

*A*nger is a passionate emotional response to a perceived evil that would cross us or hinder us from something good. It has been given to us by God for our good. It stirs us up to vigorous resistance against anything that opposes God's glory, our salvation, our real good, or the good of our neighbours. Anger is therefore good when it is used to its appointed end, in the right manner and measure. But anger may be sinful.

WHEN ANGER IS SINFUL

1. When it opposes God or good; as in the case of those who become angry with us because we seek to win them to the Lord or separate them from their sins.

2. When it disturbs our reason, and hinders us from thinking rightly.

3. When it causes us to act unbecomingly, so as to use sinful words or actions.

4. When it causes us to wrong one another by our words and deeds, or to treat others in a way in which we would not like to be treated.

5. When it is mistaken and with no just cause behind it.

6. When it is greater in measure than that which provoked the anger.

7. When it makes us unfit to do our duty to God or man.

8. When it hinders love, brotherly kindness and the good we might do for others.

9. When it encourages malice, revenge, contentions, division, oppression of those under us, and dishonour to those over us.

10. When it lasts too long, and does not cease when it has accomplished its purpose.

11. When it is used as a means to further our selfish, carnal, and sinful ends. When we are angry because our pride, profit, enjoyment, or fleshly will is crossed.

CONSIDERATIONS TO HINDER SINFUL ANGER

1. *Uncontrolled anger injures humanity and rebels against reason.* It is without reason and against reason. All passion should always be under the control of reason. It is madness, and like the crime of drunkenness, to suppress and dethrone our reason.

Sinful anger is temporary madness or drunkenness, since our reason is set aside. Remember that you are a man, and that it is a dishonour to yield to fury like an animal.

2. *God intended to govern our rational powers first, and then our lesser powers through them.* Sinful passion silences our reason, so that we are in no fit state to obey the commands of God.

3. *Sinful passion is a pain and sickness of the mind.* Will you love or cherish your disease or pain? Do you not feel yourself in pain and diseased while it is upon you? No one would want to live continually in that state. In such a state, what good can be accomplished? How can you enjoy life? What comfort is your life to you? If sinful passion is bad over a long period, how can it be good even for a short time? Do not wilfully keep so troublesome a sickness in your mind!

4. *Observe also what an enemy it is to your body.* It inflames the blood, stirs up diseases, breeds bitter displeasure in the mind, consumes our strength, and casts many into acute and chronic sickness leading even to death. And how comfortless a death this is!

5. *Observe how unlovely and displeasing you are to those who observe you.* Anger deforms the countenance, and takes away the sweet and pleasant appearance that you have when you express a calm and loving temperament. If you were always like this, would anybody love you? Would they not get out of your way (if they did not lay hands on you), as they would do to anything that is wild or mad? You would not want your picture taken while in a state of fury. Your frowns and inflamed blood mar

your countenance. Do not love that which makes you so unlovely to others.

6. *You should shun this anger because it hurts others and is an enemy to love and the good of others.* Every time you are angry you are inclined to hurt those that angered you and anyone else in the path of your fury. Anger puts hurtful thoughts in your mind and hurtful words in your mouth and entices you to strike out or do some other mischief. Nobody loves a hurtful person. Avoid so troublesome a passion.

7. *Take note of the tendency of your anger. You will find that if it is not stopped early, it will lead to the utter ruin of your brother, bloodshed, and your own damnation.* How many thousands has anger murdered or

undone! It has caused wars, and filled the world with blood and cruelty! Should your hearts give place to such a fury?

8. *Consider how much other sin stems from sinful anger.* It is like drunkenness, in which a man does not have control of himself and so lays himself open to great wickedness. How many oaths and curses does it cause every day! How many rash and sinful actions! What villainy has anger not done! It has slandered, blasphemed, reproached, falsely accused, and injured many thousands. It has murdered and ruined families, cities, and states. It has made parents kill their children, and children dishonour their parents. It has made kings oppress and murder their subjects, and subjects rebel and murder kings. What a world of sin is

committed by sinful anger throughout the world! How endless are the illustrations of it. David himself was once drawn by it to intend murdering the whole family of Nabal. All this should make it odious to us.

9. *Anger is a sin that does not leave you to sin alone.* It stirs of up others to do the same. Wrath kindles wrath, as fire kindles fire. When you are angry you will make others angry, or discontented, or troubled by your words and deeds. Once you have provoked others to anger, you do not know the extent of the sin it may lead them to. You do not have power to moderate their anger after yours has subsided. It is the devil's bellows to kindle man's corruptions and set hearts, families, and kingdoms aflame.

10. *Notice how unfit it makes you for holy duties; for prayer, meditation, or any communion with God.* This should trouble gracious souls, that anything should make us unfit to speak to God or to be employed in his worship. If indeed you do engage in prayer or other worship in a passion of anger, may not God say as Achish, king of Gath, did of David, 'Have I need of mad men?' Anger makes all of us – family, church, or society – unprepared for the worship of God. Is the family prepared for prayer when wrath has muddied and disturbed their minds? It divides Christians and churches, and causes 'confusion and every evil work' (*James* 3:15–16).

11. *It is a great dishonour to the grace of God that any servant of his should have so little self-control.* It causes the world to wonder that grace has no more force or efficacy to rule a raging passion. It is a dishonour to God when we do not possess our souls with more patience, fear of God, or self-control. Do not wrong God by so dishonouring his grace and Spirit!

12. *It is a sin against our consciences.* When one comes to oneself, in a proper frame of mind, the conscience is stricken, and the soul smitten with sorrow over the failure. The realization that we must repent afterwards should make us seek to avoid that which causes so much shame and sorrow.

OBJECTION ONE

But you may say: 'I am of a hasty choleric nature, and cannot help it.'

Answer: It is true that your temperament may be more prone to anger than other temperaments, but this cannot force you to sinful anger. Reason and will, functioning as they should, can command and master passion. If you realize your own tendency to anger, this very fact should make you even more alert and watchful concerning it.

Baxter on Anger 19

OBJECTION TWO

'But the provocation was so great that it would have angered anyone in the same circumstances!'

Answer: This is a weak argument, that you should think that some provocation can be great enough to overrule a man's reason and allow him to break the laws of God. The provocation which you call so great would have been small or non-existent to a man who had a prepared mind. You should rather say, God's majesty and dreadfulness are so great that I should not even consider offending him for any provocation. Has not God given us greater cause to obey than man can give us to sin?

OBJECTION THREE

'But it happened so fast that I had no time to deliberate or to prevent it.'

Answer: Do you not still have reason? Should not your reason be as ready to rule as passion is to rebel? Quench passion as it rises and take time for deliberation.

OBJECTION FOUR

'I am angry for a very short time, and then I am sorry for it when it is over.'

Answer: But if it is evil, even if it is short, it is still a sin and to be avoided. If you know beforehand that you will be sorry, why will you breed your own sorrow?

OBJECTION FIVE

'Everybody is angry sometimes. Even the best!'

Answer: Sin is never better because many commit it. If you observe others ruled by the grace of God, you will find that there are many who are not easily angered nor do they behave themselves furiously, railing, cursing, swearing, or doing wrong to others.

OBJECTION SIX

'I do not allow the sun to go down on my anger, so it is not sinful anger – "Let not the sun go down upon your wrath" (*Eph.* 4:26).'

Answer: The apostle never said that anger is only sinful when it continues after the sun has gone down. Paul told us not to entertain any sinful anger at all. If you should do so, however, quench it quickly and do not continue in it. Do not be angry without a cause, or go beyond the cause. When you are angry, do not sin by acting unlovingly and do not allow any evil words or deeds to spring up. Do not allow your displeasure, even if it is just, to continue. Hasten to be reconciled and to forgive.

PRACTICAL DIRECTIONS AGAINST SINFUL ANGER

DIRECTION ONE

The principal help against sinful anger lies in accustoming the soul to right attitudes.

We must live under the authority of God, with a sense of obedience to him directing our hearts. Our hearts should ever be aware of the mercy of him that forgave us and keeps us, and of the grace that assists us and heals us. Our hearts should also be mindful of the love we owe to God and man.

Such a heart is continually fortified and draws its source of preservation from within itself. Just as wrath emerges from within us, so may meekness. The main cause of wrath or meekness lies within.

DIRECTION TWO

Be careful to keep a humbled soul that does not think too highly of itself, for humility is patient and does not exaggerate injuries.

A proud man considers things as heinous or intolerable that are said or done against him. He that thinks lowly of himself sees things done or said against him as of little significance. He that magnifies himself sees offences against him also magnified. Pride is a very impatient sin: There is no pleasing a proud person, without a great deal of wit, care, and diligence. You must take as much care around him as you do around straw or gunpowder when you are holding a candle.

'By insolence comes nothing but strife' (*Prov.* 13:10.).

'An arrogant man stirs up strife' (*Prov.* 28:25, NASB).

'"Scoffer" is the name of the arrogant haughty man who acts with arrogant pride' (*Prov.* 21:24).

'Let the lying lips be mute, which speak insolently against the righteous in pride and contempt' (*Psa.* 31:18).

Humility, meekness, and patience live and die together!

DIRECTION THREE

*Be careful to avoid a worldly
and covetous mind.*

The worldly mind sets such store by
earthly things that every loss, opposition,
or injury unsettles and inflames its passions. No one can please a covetous man.
Every little trespass or crossing of his
desires cuts him to the quick and makes
him impatient.

DIRECTION FOUR

*Put a stop to your anger early,
before it goes too far.*

It is easier to control anger in its beginning. Keep an eye on the first stirrings of

your wrath and make it obey you. Your will and reason have great power in the control of anger if you will only use them according to their nature. A spark is easier to quench than a flame, and a serpent is easier to crush before it hatches out.

DIRECTION FIVE

Take control of your tongue, hands, and countenance, even if you cannot at the moment quiet or command your passion.

In this way you will avoid the greatest of the sin, and the passion itself will quickly subside because it lacks an outlet. You cannot say that it is not in your power to restrain your tongue or hands if you wish to. You must not only avoid the swearing and cursing which are marks of the profane mind, but you must also avoid multiplying words, contentions, objections, and bitter and cutting speeches, which only tend to stir up the wrath of others. Use the mild and gentle speech which is characteristic of love and tends to cool the heat that has been kindled.

'A soft answer turns away wrath, but a harsh word stirs up anger' (*Prov.* 15:1).

DIRECTION SIX

At the very least, keep silent until reason has had an opportunity to speak and you have had a chance to think.

Do not be so hasty as not to consider what you are saying or doing. A little delay will let tempers cool and allow reason to do its work.

'With patience a ruler may be persuaded, and a soft tongue will break a bone' (*Prov.* 25:15).

Patience will lessen another's anger, as well as your own. He is a madman, not a rational person, who cannot stop to think.

DIRECTION SEVEN

If you do not find it easy to quiet your anger or restrain yourself, then leave the place and company that have provoked you.

Then you will not be further inflamed by contentious words, nor exasperate others by your own angry words. When you are alone, the fire will die down.

'Leave the presence of a fool, for there you do not meet words of knowledge' (*Prov.* 14:7).

You would not stand stirring up a wasp's nest when you had already enraged the wasps.

DIRECTION EIGHT

Make it your habit to avoid talk and dispute with angry men, so far as you can do so without neglecting your duty.

Avoid all other occasions and temptations to this sin. A man that is in danger of a fever must avoid that which aggravates it. Do not go near the infected if you fear the plague. Do not stand in the sun if you are too hot already. Keep as far as possible from that which provokes you most.

DIRECTION NINE

Do not meditate upon past injuries or things that have provoked you when you are alone.

Do not allow your thoughts to feed upon these things. If you do, you will be like a devil to yourself, and tempt yourself to anger when there is no one else to do it. You will make your solitude as provocative as if you were in the midst of those who provoke you. You will stir up anger in your heart by your own imagination.

DIRECTION TEN

*Keep your minds in lively thoughts of the
exemplary meekness and patience
of Jesus Christ.*

He invites us to learn of him to be 'meek
and lowly' (*Matt.* 11:29).

'Christ also suffered for you, leaving
you an example, so that you might follow
in his steps . . . When he was reviled, he did
not revile in return; when he suffered, he
did not threaten, but continued entrusting
himself to him who judges justly' (*1 Pet.*
2:21, 23).

Remember that he has pronounced
a special blessing on the meek, that they
might 'inherit the earth' (*Matt.* 5:5).

DIRECTION ELEVEN

Live as in the presence of God; and when your passions grow bold, repress them with the reverend name of God, and remind yourself that God and his holy angels are watching you.

DIRECTION TWELVE

Look at others in their passion, and consider how unlovely they make themselves.

Think of the frowning countenances, flaming eyes, threatening, devouring looks, and harmful tencencies of those controlled by passion, and then consider whether these are desirable examples to follow.

DIRECTION THIRTEEN

When anger rises, confess your sin without delay to those around. Take the shame to yourself. Shame the sin and honour God.

Accept the shame of the sin of unruly passion, which is a dishonour to God. This is in your power to accomplish if you will, and it will be an excellent means to prevent sinful anger.

When you are tempted to sin in anger, say to those around you: 'I feel a sinful anger rising in my heart and am tempted to forget God's presence and act in a way that is not proper for his glory and speak provoking words that I know would be displeasing to him.' In confessing your temptation, you will break the force of it, and stop the fire, so that it does not progress. If you stop the progress of your passion in this way, it will be a point of honour with you not to go on in the anger you have just confessed, for your reputation will then be at stake.

This direction must be followed with wisdom, so that the confession itself does not cause others to be hardened and provoked against you, or make you look ridiculous. But with prudence and due caution, this is an excellent remedy to follow, if you are willing to do so.

DIRECTION FOURTEEN

*If you have allowed your passion to break out
and to offend or wrong others, by word or
deed, freely and speedily confess it to
them, and ask them for forgiveness.*

In confessing your fault, you may wish
to warn others not to follow your bad
example. This will do much to clear your
conscience and preserve your brother. It
will also help to overcome the effect of
your anger, and motivate you to avoid this
sin in the future. If you are so proud that
you will not do this, do not say that you
cannot help your anger, but rather that you
are unwilling to do so. A good heart will
not think this too difficult a remedy against
any sin.

DIRECTION FIFTEEN

As far as circumstances allow, go immediately to God in prayer for pardon, and grace against this sin.

Sin will not endure prayer and the presence of God. Tell him how easily your irritable heart is kindled into sinful anger. Ask him to help you by his sufficient grace. Engage Christ, your Master and Advocate, to help you; and then your soul will grow obedient and calm.

Paul prayed three times concerning his thorn in the flesh (*2 Cor.* 12:7–9); and Christ prayed in his agony. So you must pray, and pray again and again, until you find God's sufficient grace for you.

DIRECTION SIXTEEN

Make a covenant with a faithful friend to watch over you and rebuke your passions as soon as they begin to appear. Promise him that you will take it thankfully and in a proper spirit.

And keep your promise, so that your friend is not discouraged. Either you are tired of your sin and failure and willing to do all you can against it to find the victory, or you are not. If you are willing, you can do this! If you are not willing, do not pretend that you are repentant over your sin and truly want to be delivered when it is not really so. Remember also that the effects of sinful anger make it, not a small sin, but a major one.

'Be not quick in your spirit to become angry, for anger lodges in the bosom of fools' (*Eccles.* 7:9).

'Whoever is slow to anger is better than the mighty, and he who rules his spirit than he who takes a city' (*Prov.* 16:32).

'A hot-tempered man stirs up strife, but he who is slow to anger quiets contention (*Prov.* 15:18).

'Good sense makes one slow to anger, and it is his glory to overlook an offence (*Prov.* 19:11).

A BRIEF LIFE OF
RICHARD BAXTER[1]

J. C. Ryle

[1] From *Light from Old Times, or Protestant Facts and Men*, 1902; reprinted Moscow, Idaho: Charles Nolan Publishers, 2000.

BAXTER AND
HIS TIMES

*R*ichard Baxter was the son of a small landed proprietor of Eaton Constantine, in Shropshire. He was born in 1615, at Rowton, in the same county, where Richard Adeney, his mother's father, resided.

He seems to have been under religious impressions from a very early period of his life, and for this, under God, he was indebted to the training of a pious father. Shropshire was a very dark, ungodly county in those days. The ministers were generally ignorant, graceless, and unable to preach; and the people, as might be expected, were profligate, and despisers of them that were good. In Eaton Constantine, the parishioners spent the greater part of the Lord's Day in dancing round a Maypole near old Mr Baxter's door, to his great distress and annoyance. Yet even here grace triumphed over the world in the case of his son, and he was added to the noble host of those who 'serve the Lord from their youth'.

It is always interesting to observe the names of the religious books, which God is pleased to use in bringing souls to the knowledge of himself.

The books which had the most effect on Baxter were, Bunny's *Resolution;* Perkins *On Repentance, on Living and Dying Well, and on the Government of the Tongue;*

Culverwell *On Faith;* and Sibbes' *Bruised Reed.* Disease and the prospect of death did much to carry on the spiritual work within him. He says in his *Autobiography*, 'Weakness and pain helped me to study how to die. That set me on studying how to live, and that on studying the doctrines from which I must fetch my motives and my comforts.'

At the age of twenty-two he was ordained a clergyman by John Thornborough, Bishop of Worcester. He had never had the advantage of a University education. A free-school at Wroxeter, and a private tutor at Ludlow, had done something for him; and his own insatiable love of study had done a good deal more. He probably entered the ministry far better furnished with theological learning than most young men of his day. He certainly entered it with qualifications far better than a knowledge of Greek and Hebrew. He entered it truly moved by the Holy Ghost, and a converted man.

He says himself:

I knew that the want of academical honours and degrees were like to make me contemptible with the most. But yet, expecting to be so quickly in another world, the great concernment of miserable souls did prevail with me against all impediments. And being conscious of a thirsty desire of men's conscience and salvation, I resolved, that if one or two souls only might be won to God, it would easily recompense all the dishonour which, for want of titles, I might undergo from men.

From the time of his ordination to his death, Baxter's life was a constant series of strange vicissitudes, and intense physical and mental exertions.

Sometimes in prosperity and sometimes in adversity, – sometimes praised and sometimes persecuted, at one period catechizing in the lanes of Kidderminster, at another disputing with bishops in the Savoy Conference, one year writing the *Saints' Rest*, at the point of death, in a quiet country house, another year a marching chaplain in Cromwell's army, – one day offered a bishopric by Charles II, another cast out of the Church by the Act of Uniformity, – one year arguing for monarchy with Cromwell, and telling him it was a blessing, another tried before Jeffreys on a charge of seditious writing, – one time living quietly at Acton in the society of Judge Hale, at another languishing in prison under some atrocious ecclesiastical persecution, – one day having public discussions about infant baptism, with Mr Tombes, in Bewdley Church, another holding the reading-desk of Amersham Church from morning to night against the theological arguments of Antinomian dragoons in the gallery, – sometimes preaching the plainest doctrines, sometimes handling the most abstruse metaphysical points, – sometimes writing folios for the learned, sometimes writing broad-sheets for the poor, – never, perhaps, did any Christian, minister fill so many various positions; and never, certainly, did any one come out of them all with such an unblemished reputation. Always suffering under incurable disease, and seldom long out of pain, – always working his mind to the uttermost and never idle for a day, – seemingly overwhelmed with business, and yet never refusing new work, – living in the midst of the most exciting scenes, and yet holding daily intercourse with God, – not sufficiently a partisan to satisfy any side, and yet feared and courted by all, – too much of a Royalist to please the Parliamentary party, and yet too much connected with the Parliament and too holy to be popular with the Cavaliers, – too much of an Episcopalian to satisfy the violent portion of the Puritan body, and too much of a Puritan to be trusted by the bishops: never, probably, did Christian man enjoy so little rest, though serving God with a pure conscience, as did Richard Baxter.

In 1638 he began his ministry, by preaching in the Upper Church at Dudley. There he continued a year. From Dudley he removed to Bridgnorth. There he continued a year and three-quarters. From Bridgnorth he removed to Kidderminster. From thence, after two years, he retired to Coventry, at the beginning of the Commonwealth troubles, and awaited the progress of the Civil War.

From Coventry, after the battle of Naseby, he joined the Parliamentary army in the capacity of Regimental Chaplain. He took this office in the vain hope that he might do some good among the soldiers, and counteract the ambitious designs of Cromwell and his friends. He was obliged by illness to give up his chaplaincy in 1646, and lingered for some months between life and death at the hospitable houses of Sir John Coke of Melbourne, in Derbyshire, and Sir Thomas Rous of Rouslench, in Worcestershire. At the end of 1646 he returned to Kidderminster, and there continued labouring indefatigably as parish Minister for fourteen years.

In 1660 he left Kidderminster for London, and took an active part in promoting the restoration of Charles II, and was made one of the King's Chaplains. In London, he preached successively at St Dunstan's, Black Friars, and St Bride's. Shortly after this he was offered the bishopric of Hereford, but thought fit to refuse it.

In 1662 he was one of the 2,000 ministers who were turned out of the Church by the Act of Uniformity. Immediately after his ejection he married a wife who seems to have been every way worthy of him, and who was spared to be his loving and faithful companion for nineteen years. Her name was Margaret Charlton, of Apley Castle, in Shropshire. After this he lived in various places in and about London, – at Acton, Totteridge, Bloomsbury, and at last in Charterhouse Square.

The disgraceful treatment of his enemies made it almost impossible for him to have any dwelling-place. Once, at this period of his life, he was offered a Scotch bishopric, or the mastership of a Scotch university, but declined both offices.

With few exceptions, the last twenty-nine years of his life were embittered by repeated prosecutions, fines, imprisonment, and harassing controversies. When he could he preached, and when he could not preach he wrote books; but something he was always doing. The revolution and accession of William III brought him some little respite from persecution, and death at last removed the good old man to that place 'where the wicked cease from troubling and the weary are at rest', in the year 1691, and the seventy-sixth year of his age.

The day before he died, Dr Bates visited him; and on his saying some words of comfort, he replied, 'I have pain; there is no arguing against sense; but I have peace: I have peace!' Bates told him he was going to his long-desired home. He answered, 'I believe: I believe!' He expressed great willingness to die. During his sickness, when the question was asked how he did, his reply was, 'Almost well!' or else, 'Better than

I deserve to be, but not so well as I hope to be.'

Such is a brief outline of the life of one of the most distinguished Puritans who lived under the Stuarts, and one of the most devoted ministers of the gospel this country has ever seen.

We all owe a debt to the Puritans, which I trust we shall never refuse to acknowledge. We live in days when many are disposed to run them down. As we travel through life, we often hear them derided and abused as seditious, rebellious levellers in the things of Caesar, and ignorant, fanatical, hypocritical enthusiasts in the things of God. We often hear some conceited stripling fresh from college, puffed up with new-fledged views of what he calls 'apostolical succession', and proud of a little official authority, depreciating and sneering at the Puritans, as men alike destitute of learning and true religion, while, in reality he is scarcely worthy to sit at their feet and carry their books. To all such calumnies and false statements, I trust we shall never give heed.

Let us settle it down in our minds that for sound doctrine, spirituality, and learning combined, the Puritans stand at the head of English divines. With all their faults, weaknesses, and defects, they alone kept the lamp of pure, Evangelical religion burning in this country in the times of the Stuarts, – they alone prevented Laud's Popish inclinations carrying England back into the arms of Rome. It was they who fought the battle for religious freedom, of which we are reaping such fruits. It was they who crushed the wretched spirit of inquisitorial persecution which misguided high-Churchmen tried to introduce into this land.

Let us give them the honour they deserve. Let us suffer no man to speak lightly of them in our presence.

Let us remember our obligations to them, reverence their memory, stand up boldly for their reputation, and never be afraid to plead their cause. It is the cause of pure evangelical religion. It is the cause of an open Bible and liberty to meet and read and pray together. It is the cause of liberty of conscience.

OTHER BOOKS IN THE
POCKET PURITANS
SERIES

*ALSO BY
RICHARD BAXTER:*

THE REFORMED PASTOR

'Every pastor ought to have this book, and every
church member ought to see that his pastor has
it, as well as reading it himself so as to understand
the work of the pastor, and undertandingly pray
for him in that task.'

GRACE MAGAZINE

'A classic which has stood the test of time and still
comes to us fresh and pertinent more than three
hundred years since it was written . . . Richard
Baxter's *Reformed Pastor* has probably done more
to transform the lives and ministries of God's serv-
ants than any other book this side of the Reform-
ation . . . Would that we all knew the same urgency
in the face of missionary opportunities today.'

FLOODTIDE

ISBN-13: 978 0 85151 191 7
256 pp., paperback

DYING THOUGHTS

'Death for the believer is simply a doorway to heaven, but so little is taught about this great wonder that the average Christian today has vague ideas about glory and is hardly enthusiastic to get there. We should be! Baxter will remind us why. A book calculated to bring comfort, challenge, and blessing – much needed and highly recommended.'

BRITISH CHURCH NEWSPAPER

'A real gem . . . undoubtedly a book to inspire us today and challenge us to be more devoted to our Lord and His church.'

PROTESTANT TRUTH

ISBN-13: 978 0 85151 886 2
144 pp., paperback